SEEING STARS

Seeing Stars

SIMON ARMITAGE

faber and faber

First published in 2010
by Faber and Faber Ltd
Bloomsbury House
74–77 Great Russell Street
London WC1B 3DA

Typeset by Faber and Faber Ltd
Printed in England by T. J. International Ltd, Padstow, Cornwall

A CIP record for this book
is available from the British Library

ISBN 978–0–571–24990–9

2 4 6 8 10 9 7 5 3 1

for Sue

Acknowledgements

Acknowledgements and thanks are due to the editors and organisers of the following publications and projects: *Salt Magazine*, *Blackbox Manifold*, *The Literateur*, *The Rialto*, *Grist*, *PN Review*, *Poetry London*, *Yorkshire Sculpture Park* ('The Twilight Readings'), *Fiddlehead* (Canada), BBC Radio 4 'Writing the City', *Cent*, *Tatler*, *To Hell*, *Poetry Review*, *The Colour of Sound – Anthony Frost Exhibition* (Beaux Arts), *Love Poet, Carpenter – Michael Longley at Seventy* (Enitharmon), *Loops*, *TriQuarterly* (US), *The New Yorker* (US), *AGNI* (US).

Contents

SEEING STARS

The Christening

I am a sperm whale. I carry up to 2.5 tonnes of an oil-like
balm in my huge, coffin-shaped head. I have a brain the
size of a basketball, and on that basis alone am entitled to
my opinions. I am a sperm whale. When I breathe in, the
fluid in my head cools to a dense wax and I nosedive into
the depths. My song, available on audiocassette and
compact disc is a comfort to divorcees, astrologists and
those who have 'pitched the quavering canvas tent of their
thoughts on the rim of the dark crater'. The oil in my head
is of huge commercial value and has been used by NASA,
for even in the galactic emptiness of deep space it does not
freeze. I am attracted to the policies of the Green Party *on
paper* but once inside the voting booth my hand is guided
by an unseen force. Sometimes I vomit large chunks of
ambergris. My brother, Jeff, owns a camping and outdoor
clothing shop in the Lake District and is a recreational user
of cannabis. Customers who bought books about me also
bought *Do Whales Have Belly Buttons?* by Melvin Berger
and street maps of Cardiff. In many ways I have *seen it all*.
I keep no pets. Lying motionless on the surface I am said
to be 'logging', and 'lobtailing' when I turn and offer my
great slow fluke to the horizon. Don't be taken in by the
dolphins and their winning smiles, they are the pickpockets
of the ocean, the gypsy children of the open waters and
they are laughing all the way to Atlantis. On the basis of
'finders keepers' I believe the Elgin Marbles should
remain the property of the British Crown. I am my own
God – why shouldn't I be? The first people to open me up
thought my head was full of sperm, but they were men, and
had lived without women for many weeks, and were far
from home. Stuff comes blurting out.

An Accommodation

—— and I both agreed that something had to change,
but I was still stunned and not a little hurt when I
staggered home one evening to find she'd draped a
net curtain slap bang down the middle of our home.
She said, 'I'm over here and you're over there, and
from now on that's how it's going to be.' It was a
small house, not much more than a single room,
which made for one or two practical problems.
Like the fridge was on my side and the oven was on
hers. And she had the bed while I slept fully
clothed in the inflatable chair. Also there was a
Hüsker Dü CD on her half of the border which I
wouldn't have minded hearing again for old times'
sake, and her winter coat stayed hanging on the
door in my domain. But the net was the net, and we
didn't so much as pass a single word through its
sacred veil, let alone send a hand crawling beneath
it, or, God forbid, yank it aside and go marching
across the line. Some nights she'd bring men back,
deadbeats, incompatible, not fit to kiss the heel of
her shoe. But it couldn't have been easy for her
either, watching me mooch about like a ghost,
seeing me crashing around in the empty bottles and
cans. And there were good times too, sitting side by
side on the old settee, the curtain between us, the
TV in her sector but angled towards me, taking me
into account.

Over the years the moths moved in, got a taste for
the net, so it came to resemble a giant web, like a
thing made of actual holes strung together by fine,

nervous threads. But there it remained, and remains to this day, this tattered shroud, this ravaged lace suspended between our lives, keeping us inseparable and betrothed.

The Cuckoo

When James Cameron was a young man, this happened
to him. After his eighteenth birthday party had come to
an end and the guests had disappeared wearing colourful
hats and clutching cubes of Battenberg cake wrapped in
paper napkins, James's mother sat him down at the
breakfast bar. The smell of snuffed candles and
discharged party poppers floated in the air. 'James, I'm
not your mother,' she told him. 'What?' he managed to
croak. 'I work for the government and my contract
comes to an end today.' 'Does dad know?' asked the
bewildered James. 'He's not your father. Don't be cross
with us, we're only doing our job.' James felt like a gold
tooth sent flying through the air in a fist fight. 'What
about my brother, Peter, and all the family?' 'Actors,'
she said, very matter-of-factly. 'I don't believe you. Not
auntie Madge.' 'Especially her. She went to drama
school. She was always a tad Shakespearian for my taste
but some people like that approach.' The small tear in
James's eye, like a baby snail, finally emerged from its
shell. 'Will you leave me?' he asked. She said, 'There's
a taxi coming in half an hour. I've left a chilli con carne
in the fridge and there's a stack of pizzas in the freezer.
Pepperoni – the ones you like. We're opening a bed and
breakfast place on the east coast. Actually it's a safe-
house for political prisoners – I can tell you that because
I know you won't repeat it.' Suddenly she looked like the
meanest woman who ever lived, though of course he
loved her very being.

James went outside. His best friend, Snoobie, and Carla,
his girlfriend, were leaning on the wall with suitcases in

their hands. Carla was wearing sunglasses and passing a piece of chewing gum from one side of her mouth to the other. 'Not you two as well?' said James, despairingly. ''Fraid so,' said Snoobie. 'Anyway, take care. I've been offered a small part in a play at the Palace Theatre in Watford and there's a read through tomorrow morning. She's off to Los Angeles, aren't you, Carla?' 'Hollywood,' she said, still chewing the gum. James said, 'Didn't it mean anything, Carla? Not even that time behind the taxi rank after the Microdisney concert?' 'Dunno,' she shrugged. 'I'd have to check the file.' James could have punched a hole in her chest and ripped out the poisonous blowfish of her heart. He walked heavily up to the paddock. If he'd been a smoker who'd quit, now would have been the time to start again. If he'd been carrying a loaded firearm in his pocket he might have put that to his lips as well. Then a bird fell out of the sky and landed just a yard or so from his feet. A cuckoo. It flapped a few times and died. However tormented or shabby you're feeling, however low your spirits, thought James, there's always someone worse off. His mother had taught him that. It was then he noticed the tiny electric motor inside the bird's belly, and the wires under its wings, and the broken spring sticking out of its mouth.

Back in the Early Days of the Twenty-First Century

Back in the early days of the twenty-first century I was
working as a balloon seller on the baked and crumbling
streets of downtown Mumbai. It was lowly work for a
man like me with a sensitive nature and visionary dreams,
but at least I wasn't moping around like a zombie,
tapping the windows of taxis and limousines with a
broken fingernail, begging for biscuits and change.
Besides which, these were no ordinary inflatables, but
gargantuan things, like gentle, alien beings. To drum up
business I'd fill one with air and slap the flat of my hand
on the quivering skin, the sound booming out among
passing tourists, reverberating through body and soul.

It was a sticky and slow Thursday in March when he
crossed the road towards me, that man in his seersucker
suit, and chose a purple balloon from the bag, lifted it
with his little finger like evidence found at the scene of
some filthy crime, and said, 'How much for this?' We
haggled and he bargained hard, drove me down to my
lowest price, which was two rupees, then he said, 'OK,
but I want it blowing up.' 'No, sir,' I said, 'that price
is without air.' 'Blowing up, buddy, right to the top, or
I'm walking away,' said the man in the seersucker suit.
Trade had been slack that day. In fact in ten sun-
strangled hours this was my only nibble, and to walk
home with empty pockets is to follow the hearse, so they
say. So I exhaled at great length, breathed the air of
existence into that purple blimp, and to this day I wish I
had not. For with that breath my soul was sold, and all
for the price of a cup of betel nuts or a lighted candle
placed in the lap of the elephant god.

And his lazy daughter danced with me once and left me
to slouch and gag in the stinking womb of my own stale
breath. Then his fat boy bundled me straight to his room,
and when I wouldn't yield to his two-fisted punches and
flying bicycle kicks, all the spite of puberty coursed
through the veins in his neck, and the light in his eye
shrank to a white-hot, pin-sharp, diamond-tipped point.

Michael

So George has this theory: the first thing we ever steal, when we're young, is a symbol of what we become later in life, when we grow up. Example: when he was nine George stole a Mont Blanc fountain pen from a fancy gift shop in a hotel lobby – now he's an award-winning novelist. We test the theory around the table and it seems to add up. Clint stole a bottle of cooking sherry, now he owns a tapas bar. Kirsty's an investment banker and she stole money from her mother's purse. Tod took a Curly Wurly and he's morbidly obese. Claude says he never stole anything in his whole life, and he's an actor i.e. unemployed. Derek says, 'But wait a second, I stole a blue Smurf on a polythene parachute.' And Kirsty says, 'So what more proof do we need, Derek?'

Every third Saturday in the month I collect my son from his mother's house and we take off, sometimes to the dog track, sometimes into the great outdoors. Last week we headed into the Eastern Fells to spend a night under the stars and to get some quality time together, father and son. With nothing more than a worm, a bent nail and a thread of cotton we caught a small, ugly-looking fish; I was all for tossing it back in the lake, but Luke surprised me by slapping it dead on a flat stone, slitting its belly and washing out its guts in the stream. Then he cooked it over a fire of brushwood and dead leaves, and for all the thinness of its flesh and the annoying pins and needles of its bones, it made an honest meal. Later on, as it dropped dark, we bedded down in an old deer shelter on the side of the hill. There was a hole in the roof. Lying there on our backs, it was as if we were looking into the inky blue

eyeball of the galaxy itself, and the darker it got, the more
the eyeball appeared to be staring back. Remembering
George's theory, I said to Luke, 'So what do you think
you'll be, when you grow up?' He was barely awake,
but from somewhere in his sinking thoughts and with a
drowsy voice he said, 'I'm going to be an executioner.'
Now the hole in the roof was an ear, the ear of the
universe, exceptionally interested in my very next words.
I sat up, rummaged about in the rucksack, struck a match
and said, 'Hold on a minute, son, you're talking about
taking a person's life. Why would you want to say a
thing like that?' Without even opening his eyes he said,
'But I'm sure I could do it. Pull the hood over someone's
head, squeeze the syringe, flick the switch, whatever.
You know, if they'd done wrong. Now go to sleep, dad.'

I'll Be There to Love and Comfort You

The couple next door were testing the structural fabric of the house with their difference of opinion. 'I can't take much more of this,' I said to Mimi my wife. Right then there was another almighty crash, as if every pan in the kitchen had clattered to the tiled floor. Mimi said, 'Try to relax. Take one of your tablets.' She brewed a pot of camomile tea and we retired to bed. But the pounding and caterwauling carried on right into the small hours. I was dreaming that the mother of all asteroids was locked on a collision course with planet Earth, when unbelievably a fist came thumping through the bedroom wall just above the headboard. In the metallic light of the full moon I saw the bloody knuckles and a cobweb tattoo on the flap of skin between finger and thumb, before the fist withdrew. Mimi's face was powdered with dirt and dust, but she didn't wake. She looked like a corpse pulled from the rubble of an earthquake after five days in a faraway country famous only for its paper kites.

I peered through the hole in the wall. It was dark on the other side, with just occasional flashes of purple or green light, like those weird electrically-powered life forms zipping around in the ocean depths. There was a rustling noise, like something stirring in a nest of straw, then a voice, a voice no bigger than a sixpence, crying for help. Now Mimi was right next to me. 'It's her,' she said. I said, 'Don't be crazy, Mimi, she'd be twenty-four by now.' 'It's her I tell you. Get her back, do you hear me? GET HER BACK.' I rolled up my pyjama sleeve and pushed my arm into the hole, first to my elbow, then as far as my shoulder and neck. The air beyond was clammy and damp, as if I'd reached into a nineteenth-century London street in late November, fog rolling in up the river, a cough in a doorway. Mimi was out of her mind by now. My right cheek and my ear were flat to the wall. Then slowly but slowly I opened my fist to the unknown. And out of the void, slowly but slowly it came: the pulsing starfish of a child's hand, swimming and swimming and coming to settle on my upturned palm.

The English Astronaut

He splashed down in rough seas off Spurn Point.
I watched through a coin-op telescope jammed
with a lollipop stick as a trawler fished him out
of the waves and ferried him back to Mission
Control on a trading estate near the Humber Bridge.
He spoke with a mild voice: yes, it was good to be
home; he'd missed his wife, the kids, couldn't wait
for a shave and a hot bath. 'Are there any more
questions?' No, there were not.

I followed him in his Honda Accord to a Little
Chef on the A1, took the table opposite, watched
him order the all-day breakfast and a pot of tea.
'You need to go outside to do that,' said the
waitress when he lit a cigarette. He read the paper,
started the crossword, poked at the black pudding
with his fork. Then he stared through the window
for long unbroken minutes at a time, but only at the
busy road, never the sky. And his face was not the
moon. And his hands were not the hands of a man
who had held between finger and thumb the blue
planet, and lifted it up to his watchmaker's eye.

Hop In, Dennis

A man was hitching a lift on the slip road of the A16 just outside Calais. Despite his sharp, chiselled features and a certain desperation to his body language, I felt compelled to pick him up, so I pulled across and rolled down the window. He stuck his face in the car and said, 'I am Dennis Bergkamp, player of football for Arsenal. Tonight we have game in Luxembourg but because I am fear of flying I am travel overland. Then I have big argument with chauffeur and here he drops me. Can you help?' 'Hop in, Dennis,' I said. He threw his kit in the back and buckled up next to me. 'So what was the barney about?' I asked him. Dennis sighed and shook his classical-looking head. 'He was ignoramus. He was dismissive of great Dutch master Vermeer and says Rembrandt was homosexual.' 'Well you'll hear no such complaints from me,' I assured him. We motored along and the landscape just zipped by. And despite some of the niggles and tetchiness which crept into Dennis's game during the latter part of his career, he was a perfect gentleman and the complete travelling companion. For example, he limited himself to no more than four wine gums from the bag which gaped open between us, and was witty and illuminating without ever resorting to name-dropping or dressing-room gossip.

Near the Belgian border a note of tiredness entered Dennis's voice, so to soothe him to sleep I skipped from Classic Rock to Easy Listening. It wasn't until we were approaching the outskirts of the city that he stirred and looked at his Rolex. 'It will sure be a tight one,' he said. 'Why don't you get changed in the car and I'll drop you off at the ground?' I suggested. 'Good plan,' he said, and wriggled into the back. In the corner of my eye he was a contortion of red and white, like Santa Claus in a badger trap, though of course I afforded him complete privacy, because like most professionally trained drivers I use only the wing mirrors, never the rear view. Pretty swiftly he dropped into the seat beside me, being careful not to scratch the console with his studs. 'Here's the stadium,' I said, turning into a crowded boulevard awash with flags and scarves. Dennis jogged away towards a turnstile, through which the brilliance of the floodlights shone like the light from a distant galaxy.

And it's now that I have to confess that Mr Bergkamp was only one of dozens of Dennises to have found their way into the passenger seat of my mid-range saloon. Dennis Healey, Dennis Hopper, Dennis Potter, Dennis Lillee, the underrated record producer Dennis Bovell, and many, many more. I once drove Dennis Thatcher from Leicester Forest East service station to Ludlow races and he wasn't a moment's bother, though I did have to ask him to refrain from smoking, and of course not to breathe one word about the woman who introduced rabies to South Yorkshire.

Upon Opening the Chest Freezer

From the last snowfall of winter to settle on
the hills Damien likes to roll up a ginormous
snowball then store it in the chest freezer in
the pantry for one of his little stunts. Come
high summer, in that thin membrane of night
which divides one long day from the next,
he'll drive out in the van and deposit his
snowball at a bus stop or crossroads or at the
door of a parish church. Then from a discreet
distance, using the telescopic lens, he'll snap
away with the Nikon, documenting the
awestruck citizenry who swarm around his
miracle of meteorology, who look upon such
mighty works bewildered and amazed.

Damien, I'm through playing housewife to your
'art' and this brief story-poem is to tell you
I'm leaving. I'm gaffer-taping it to the inside
of the freezer lid; if you're reading it, you're
staring into the steaming abyss where nothing
remains but a packet of boneless chicken thighs
and a scattering of petis pois, as hard as bullets
and bruised purple by frost. At first it was just
a scoop here and a scraping there, slush puppies
for next door's kids, a lemon sorbet after the
Sunday roast, an ice pack once in a while for my
tired flesh, then margaritas for that gaggle of
sycophants you rolled home with one night,
until the day dawned when there wasn't so
much as a snowflake left. And I need for you
now to lean into the void and feel for yourself
the true scald of Antarctica's breath.

Seeing Stars

A young, sweet-looking couple came into my pharmacy.
The woman said, 'I'd like this hairbrush, please. Oh, and
a packet of sugar-free chewing gum. Oh, and I'll take one
of these as well,' she added, pointing to a pregnancy-
testing kit on the counter. I slipped it into a paper bag, and
as I was handing back her change I winked at her and said,
'Fingers crossed!' 'What did you say?' asked the man.
'I was just wishing you luck,' I said. 'Why don't you
mind your own business, pal,' he hissed. 'Or is it giving
you a big hard-on, thinking about my girl dropping her
knickers and pissing on one of those plastic sticks?' A boom-
ing, cavernous emptiness expanded inside me – I felt like
Gaping Ghyll on the one day of the year they open it
up to the public. 'You're right, sir,' I said. 'I've
overstepped the mark. I'm normally a model of discretion
and tact, but not only have I embarrassed you and your
good lady, I've brought shame on the ancient art of the
apothecary. Please, by way of recompense, choose
something and take it, free of charge.' The man said,
'Give me some speed.' 'Er, I was thinking more like a
packet of corn plasters or a pair of nail scissors. What
about one of these barley sugar sticks – they're very good for
nausea?' 'Just get me the amphetamine sulphate,' he
fumed. Then the woman said, 'Yeah, and I'll take a few
grams of heroin. The pure stuff you give to people in
exquisite pain. And you can throw in a syringe while
you're at it.' 'But think of the baby,' I blurted out.

When people have received a blow to the head they often
talk about 'seeing stars', and as a man of science I have
always been careful to avoid the casual use of metaphor

and hyperbole. But I saw stars that day. Whole galaxies of stars, and planets orbiting around them, each one capable of sustaining life as we know it. I waved from the porthole of my interstellar rocket as I hurtled past, and from inside their watery cocoons millions of helpless half-formed creatures with doughy faces and pink translucent fingers waved back.

Last Words

C was bitten on her ring finger by a teensy orange spider hiding inside a washed-and-ready-to-eat packet of sliced courgettes imported from Kenya. The finger swelled and tightened; how could the epidermis stretch so far without tearing apart? But the real problem was in her toes: pretty soon she lost all feeling in her feet and dropped to the floor, and moment by moment the numbness increased as if molten lead were flowing through her veins to her lower limbs. However, her mind remained clear, and with great foresight she thumped the leg of the kitchen table with the outside of her fist, causing the telephone handset to jump from the docking station and fall safely into the hairy tartan blanket in the wicker dog basket. She called her brother, Sandy. Sandy's voice said, 'Hi, I'm at the golf course, leave a message.' She called her mother. Her mother said, 'Forget the spider, where's that pastry brush I lent you, and the silver candlesticks you borrowed to impress that boss of yours at one of your fancy-pants dinner parties? Where will it all end, C? It'll be the melon baller next, then the ice cream scoop, and soon I'll have nothing. Do you hear me? Nothing. God knows I didn't bring you up to be a thief but you have a problem with honesty, C, you really do. Did you find a man yet? Now leave me alone, I can hear the nurse coming.' C's dog padded over and licked her chin, then went back into the living room to watch daytime TV.

C lay on the tiles on the kitchen floor for a few cold, quiet minutes, considering the ever after. Then with her good hand she punched a long, random number into the keypad, eleven or twelve digits. After a lot of clicking and crackling, it rang. 'Who is this?' said a man. 'My name's C and I'm dying from a spider bite,' she said, and described the incident with the insect and the pre-packed salad vegetables. The man said, 'I'm dying too. I've been adrift in an inflated inner tube in the Indian Ocean for six days now, and the end is near. I think a shark took my leg but I daren't look.' 'Why don't you call for help?' she asked. 'Why don't you?' he replied. His name was Dean. They chatted for a while, not caring a hoot about the cost of premium-rate international calls during peak periods. 'Is it dark there?' C wanted to know. 'Yes. Are you married?' asked Dean. C replied, 'I've had no luck with men, even though I'm a lovely person and I've taken good care of my body.' 'What's your best feature?' 'My laugh,' said C, laughing. 'And my lips, which have never received the attention they deserve.' The poison had reached as far as her windpipe and was tightening around her throat. Dean said, 'Do you think we could have made it together?' 'I think so,' she whispered. 'I don't like courgettes,' Dean joked, and those were his last words. 'I would have done broccoli instead,' she breathed, 'or even cauliflower. Whatever you asked for I would have made.'

There was a horrible pause as we sat there wondering whether or not to applaud, then the curtains closed.

My Difference

I've been writing a lot of poems recently about my
difference but my tutor isn't impressed. He hasn't said as
much, yet it's clear that as far as he's concerned my
difference doesn't *cut much ice*. He wants me to dress my
difference with tinsel and bells and flashing lights, or sit it
on a float and drive it through town at the head of the May
Day Parade. 'Tell me one interesting fact about your
difference,' he says, so I tell him about the time I lost my
difference down the plughole in a Bournemouth guesthouse
and had to fish it back with a paperclip on a length of
dental floss. He says, 'Er, that's not really what I had in
mind, Henry.' Basically he needs my difference to die in a
crash, or be ritually amputated in a civil war. Then he
shows me a prize-winning poem (one of his own in fact)
about a set of twins whose differences were swapped at
birth by a childless midwife, and who grew up with the
wrong differences, one in the bosom of the Saudi Royal
Family and the other beneath the 'jackboot of poverty', and
who met in later life only to discover their that differences
were exactly the same. He wants me to lock my difference
in a coal cellar until it comes of age then take it outside and
reverse over with the ride-on mower, thus making my
difference *very different indeed*, or auction my difference in
the global marketplace, or film it getting a 'happy slapping'
in a busy street, or scream the details of my difference into
the rabbit hole of the cosmos hoping to bend the ear of
creation itself. I tell him I once swallowed my difference
without water on an empty stomach, but he isn't listening
any more. He's quoting some chap who went at his
difference with a pair of pinking shears. He's talking about
such and such a poet who threw his difference in front of

the royal train, or had it beaten from him by plain-clothed officers and rendered down into potting compost or wallpaper paste, or set fire to his difference on primetime national TV. And when I plead with him that no matter how small and pitiful my difference might seem to him, to me it makes all the difference in the world, he looks at me with an expression of complete and undisguised and irreversible indifference.

The Accident

Leo burnt his hand very badly on a jet of steam
which hissed from his toasted pitta bread as he
opened it up with a knife. The visiting nurse said,
'Are you sure you haven't been beating up your
wife?' 'Excuse me?' said Leo. 'Are you sure you
didn't sustain this injury during the course of
physically assaulting your wife?' questioned the
nurse. Leo was shocked. 'It's a burn,' he said.
'Of course it's a burn, but who's to say she
wasn't defending herself with a steam iron or a
frying pan? Do you cook your own meals, sir, or
do you insist on your wife doing the housework?'
Leo was flabbergasted. 'I'm not even married,'
he said. 'Yeah, right, and I'm the Angel of the
North,' she said, throwing him a roll of lint as she
barged out of the house and slammed the door
behind her.

Leo really wasn't married. His friends were
married. Both of them. One was even divorced.
But Leo was a bachelor and not at all happy with
the situation. Bachelor – the word tasted like
diesel in his mouth. However, that night in the
pub he met Jacqueline, a young blind woman
from York, and they talked for a while on the
subject of Easter Island, about which neither of
them knew anything, and after an hour they were
still talking, and a few moments later their knees
touched under the wooden table. For him it was
like a parachute opening. For her it was like
something involving an artichoke. He lifted his

hopelessly bandaged hand to within a millimetre of her cheek and said, 'Jacqueline, I'll never hurt you. I wouldn't do that. Everything's going to be all right from now on and you're safe. Jackie, I love you. Do you understand?'

Aviators

They'd overbooked the plane. 'At this moment in time,'
announced the agent at the counter, 'Rainbow Airlines
is offering one hundred pounds or a free return flight to
any passenger willing to stand down.' A small man in a
cheap suit and Bart Simpson socks scratched his ankle.
'One hundred and fifty pounds,' she announced, fifteen
minutes later. Nobody moved. 'Two hundred?' From
nowhere, this neat-looking chap in a blue flannel jacket
and shiny shoes loomed over the desk and said, 'I'll take
the money.' 'But you're the pilot,' she said, then added,
'Sir,' as if she'd walked into a Japanese house and
forgotten to take off her shoes. The pilot whispered,
'Listen, I need that money. I'm behind on my mortgage
payments because my wife's a gambler. I've got two
sons at naval college – the hats alone cost a small fortune
– and I'm being blackmailed by a pimp in Stockport. Let
me take the two hundred, you'd be saving my life.'

I'd been sitting within earshot, next to the stand-up
ashtray. 'Give him the money,' I said. 'Who are you?'
asked Dorothy (she was wearing a plastic name-badge
with gold letters). 'Dorothy, I'm George,' I said, 'and
clearly this man's in pain. I don't want him going all
gooey midway over the English Channel. I once heard
sobbing coming from the cabin of a Jumbo Jet at thirty-
three thousand feet, and it sounded like the laughter of
Beelzebub.' 'But who'll fly the plane?' she wanted to
know. 'Why me, of course.' I opened my mouth so she
could see how good my teeth were – like pilot's teeth.
'Do you have a licence?' she asked. I said, 'Details,
always details. Dorothy, it's time to let go a little, to trust

in the unexplained. Time to open your mind to the infinite.' By now my hand was resting on hers, and a small crowd of passengers had gathered around, nodding and patting me on the back. 'Good for you, George,' said a backpacker with a leather shoelace knotted around his wrist. It was biblical, or like the end of a family film during the time of innocence. I said, 'Dorothy, give me the keys to the cockpit, and let's get this baby in the air.'

15:30 by the Elephant House

'Let's get married at the zoo!' exclaimed Scott. 'Perfect,' said Charlene. They found the name of a humanist minister in the Yellow Pages and he arranged to meet them at 15:30 by the elephant house. 'Are you sure you wouldn't prefer the glass wall of the penguin tank as a backdrop?' asked the minister. 'They're so vivacious and life-affirming.' 'No, here's fine,' said Scott. 'Perfect,' agreed Charlene. 'Then let's begin. Do you, Scott, believe that friendship and decency underpin the essence of humanity?' 'I do,' said Scott, removing a stray hair clinging to Charlene's lip. 'And do you, Charlene, agree to hand over the universe to future generations in an improved and morally enhanced condition?' 'I do,' said Charlene, 'I most truthfully do.' But before the minister could pronounce them husband and wife, a hulking brute of a man in dirty waders and a peaked cap came galumphing towards them, bellowing, 'What the bloody hell fire is going on here?' The minister had sidled away very smartly and was pretending to admire the aardvark. 'We're getting married,' said Scott. 'Not in my zoo you're not,' said the man. 'Have you no respect for these creatures, flaunting your humanness in front of them? Can't you see how defeated and ashamed they are? Have you looked the orang-utan in the face?' Scott said, 'But we're nature lovers.' The zookeeper guffawed. 'You're a pair of hypocrites. Now fuck off.' Charlene's heart sank to the sea bed of her stomach. She hadn't wanted to hear a word like that on her wedding day. 'Go on, leave this place. The capybara needs its toenails cutting, and when I come back I want to find you supremacists gone.'

It rained and there were no taxis. The silk dress Charlene had ordered from a tailor in Wushi began to perish in front of her eyes, and the scar on his back where Scott had once been treated for shingles began to throb and burn. Back in the house they argued like flamethrowers. But later, after two bottles of chilled Veuve Clicquot and a tray of Dublin Bay oysters in bison grass vodka, they pushed the coffee table to one side and in front of a glowing fire dispensed with restraint for the first time in their lives. For the heart shall never relinquish its claim on the crown, and from love's furnace shall the golden infant be born. And I should know, because my name is Sean Wain, Australian test cricketer, peerless spinner of a red leather ball and their beautiful bastard son.

An Obituary

Stealing from his mother's house, Edward came across a handwritten note tucked away in a scallop-shell purse.

'As a child, Edward liked to climb trees in the plantation and make dams in the stream at the foot of the garden, and once carved a toy rifle out of a table leg. But right from the very beginning there was a craving emptiness in Edward's life. Board games and soft toys, space-hoppers and bikes – the more it was given the deeper and wider it grew. All sweetness was rancid on Edward's tongue and all teachers and doctors were assassins and spies. All handshakes were tentacles, all compliments were veiled threats, all statements and assessments were worthless confessions obtained under torture, all care plans were Byzantine conspiracies of evil intent. Awake and asleep Edward stalked the battlements alone, meeting the emissaries of peace with the point of a bayonet, beading friendship in the crosshairs of suspicion, scanning the open plane from the watchtower so as to ride out and beat until dead the first flames of tenderness or the sparks of love. He is survived by his mother, Eleanor, from whom he took everything, but who would give it all again just to let him scream his agonies into her face or pound his fury into her breast one final time. He left no note.'

Edward opened the wardrobe, which was empty except for the greatcoat, which slumped towards him then engulfed him as he hauled it from the rail. The huge, overburdening coat with its stiff, turf-like cloth, and its triceratops collar, and its mineshaft pockets, and the drunken punches of its flailing sleeves. Through the neat bullet hole in the back, daylight looked distant and pinched, like the world through a dusty telescope held back-to-front to the eye. And there Edward wept, crouched in the foxhole, huddled in a ball under the greatcoat, draped in the flag.

Knowing What We Know Now

The elf said to Kevin, 'You're probably wondering why
I'm sitting here at your breakfast table this morning,
helping myself to your condiments. Kevin, I'm here to
make you a very special offer – let's call it a once-in-a-
lifetime opportunity. Today you're forty-four years and
thirty-six days old, and that's exactly how long you've got
left! Let me save you the mental arithmetic: you're going
to live till you're eighty-eight years and seventy-two days,
and you've just crossed the halfway line. It's what we
elves like to call "the tipping point". So, Kevin, as of now,
you can either carry on regardless and pretend we never
met. Or say the word, and I can flip the hourglass on its
head. Do you see what I'm saying? So instead of getting
older you'll be heading back in the other direction. I've got
all the forms – you just sign here, here and here and it's
goodbye incontinence, hello Ibiza! What do you say,
Kevin?'

The arthritis in Kevin's shoulder had been bothering him
of late, and the prospect of revitalising his tired and aching
joints was tantalising to say the least. Imagine crusading
once again through the unconquered landscapes of early
manhood, knowing what he knew now. But what about
Annie, the woman he loved, the *only* woman he'd loved in
his whole life? Could he really go swanning around with a
young man's intentions and a fashionable T-shirt while she
slipped away towards undignified infirmity and toothless
old age? How cowardly, to let her walk death's shadowy
footpath alone, thus betraying his every promise to her,
thus breaking every vow. And an image formed in his
mind – Annie with ghostly hair and faraway eyes, cradling

him in her limp, skinny arms, roses in a vase on the bedside table next to the tissues and ventilator, his flawless cheek against her grey cotton gown, his tiny mouth moving hungrily towards her sunken breast. 'I won't do it. Because of my Annie,' said Kevin, emphatically. The elf said, 'Kevin, you're a gentleman, and God knows there aren't many of them around. And your Annie, she's one in a million.' He wiped a few crumbs of crispbread from the corner of his mouth and added, 'No two ways about it, had the pleasure of breakfasting with her just a few months ago. A stunning, captivating woman. And looking younger every day.' Then with a shuffle of his silver slippers on the hardwood floor, he was gone.

The Experience

I hadn't meant to go grave robbing with Richard Dawkins
but he can be very persuasive. 'Do you believe in God?'
he asked. 'I don't know,' I said. He said, 'Right, so get
in the car.' We cruised around the cemetery with the
headlights off. 'Here we go,' he said, pointing to a plot
edged with clean, almost luminous white stone. I said,
'Doesn't it look sort of . . .' 'Sort of what?' 'Sort of
fresh?' I said. 'Pass me the shovel,' he said. Then he
threw a square of canvas over the headstone, saying,
'Don't read it. It makes it personal.' He did all the
digging, holding the torch in his mouth as he chopped and
sliced at the dirt around his feet. 'What the hell are you
doing?' he shouted from somewhere down in the soil.
'Eating a sandwich,' I said. 'Bacon and avocado. Want
one?' 'For Christ sake, Terry, this is a serious business,
not the bloody church picnic,' he said, as a shower of dirt
came arcing over his shoulder.

After about half an hour of toil I heard the sound of metal
on wood. 'Bingo,' he said. Then a moment or two later,
'Oh, you're not going to like this, Terry.' 'What?' I said,
peering over the edge. Richard Dawkins's eyes were about
level with my toes. 'It's quite small,' he said. He
uncovered the outline of the coffin lid with his boot. It was
barely more than a yard long and a couple of feet wide. I
felt the bacon and avocado disagreeing with one another.
'Do you believe in God?' he said. I shrugged my
shoulders. 'Pass me the jemmy,' he said. The lid
splintered around the nail heads; beneath the varnish the
coffin was nothing but cheap chipboard. The day I found
little Harry in the bath, one eye was closed and the other

definitely wasn't. Flying fish can't really fly. With both feet on the crowbar Richard Dawkins bounced up and down until the coffin popped open. But lying still and snug in the blue satin of the upholstered interior was a goose. A Canada Goose, I think, the ones with the white chinstrap, though it was hard to be certain because its throat had been cut and its rubber-looking feet were tied together with gardening twine. Richard Dawkins leaned back against the wall of the grave and shook his head. With a philosophical note in my voice I said, 'What did you come here for, Richard Dawkins?' He said, 'Watches, jewellery, cash. A christening cup, maybe. What about you?' 'I thought it might give me something to write about,' I replied. 'Well, Samuel Taylor Coleridge, we've got a murdered goose in a child's coffin in the middle of the night, and mud on our boots. How would you finish this one?' he said. I looked around, trying to think of a way out of this big ugly mess. Then I said, 'I've got it. What if we see the vicar over there, under the yew tree, looking at us? He stares at us and we stare back, but after a while we realise it isn't the vicar at all. It's a fox. You know, with the white bib of fur around its neck, which we thought was a collar. A silent, man-size fox in a dark frockcoat and long black gloves, standing up on his hind legs, watching.'

Collaborators

A small, heavy man stuck his perfectly bald head
through the open door of Bastian's barber's shop and
said, 'Do I need an appointment or can you squeeze
me in?' Trade had been brisk that morning and
Bastian had only just put his feet up to read the paper.
'Er, take a seat,' said Bastian. The man threw his
jacket onto the hat stand and jumped in the chair.
'What can I do you for?' asked Bastian. His bald
head was as pink as a pig. It was also a mirrorball set
with a hundred glistening beads of sweat. 'You can
get this fringe out of my eyes for a start,' said the
man. 'It's like trekking through Borneo!' Bastian
giggled nervously. 'Something funny?' the man said.
'No, nothing, just a tickly cough,' said Bastian. He
produced his scissors from the pouch pocket of his
apron and made a few tentative snips at the fresh air
in front of the man's eyes. 'Better already,' said the
man. 'And take some off the top and around the ears,
will you?' Bastian embarked on a slow orbit of the
man's naked cranium, darting in and out with the
scissors, even dusting a few imaginary hairs off his
shoulders with the brush. 'So good, so good,' the
man muttered, then, 'Didn't realise how out of hand it
had got till I caught sight of myself in the butcher's
window this morning. Said to myself – now there's
a head in need of a haircut.' Bastian was getting the
hang of it now, warming to the task. 'What about
the ponytail?' he asked. 'Yeah, fuck it, why not,'
said the man after hesitating a moment. With his
biggest, shiniest scissors Bastian ceremonially lopped
off the nonexistent twist of hair from behind the

man's head then held it up for inspection between his finger and thumb. 'Excuse me for being bold, sir, but might I suggest a complete shave? Extreme, I know, but very cleansing in this sultry autumn heat, and increasingly popular with some of my younger clientele.' The man, who was fifty if he was a day, said, 'Even with men as young as me?' 'It seems to be the fashionable choice, sir,' said Bastian. 'Do it,' said the man. He gripped the metal arms of the chair as Bastian buzzed around him with the electric clippers then finished the job with the cutthroat razor, the stropped blade passing deliriously close to the scalp. 'It's a revelation,' the customer proclaimed upon opening his eyes, and for a minute or so he sat there like a chimp with a mirror, dabbing his nude skull with astonished fingers, genuine in his disbelief. Then he paid Bastian with pretend money and set off down the street whistling a happy song.

By the time he came to lock the door and put the CLOSED sign in the window later that evening, Bastian had forgotten the hairless customer. But after sweeping the linoleum and shaking the curls and locks of a day's work into the dustbin in the alleyway, he was dumbfounded to notice a long, golden ponytail tied neatly with twine, then to find nails and thorns, and also what looked like teeth, and the suggestion of a small black moustache.

Ricky Wilson Couldn't Sleep

He got up and went for a walk. It was 4 o'clock in the morning. There was no one around except for a drunk sleeping it off in the doorway of Vidal Sassoon. Then an orange came rolling towards Ricky down Albion Street. It trundled in his direction before clipping a kerbstone and jumping straight into his hands. The orange was dusty and slightly misshapen from its journey, but after a quick polish with his cravat and a bit of moulding in his hands, the fruit was restored. He stared at it under the glow of the streetlamps. It looked very appealing indeed. In fact at that second Ricky was seized with the overpowering notion that all his bodily cravings could be satisfied by the quenching juice and zesty pulp of that ample citrus fruit sitting in his palm, so without hesitation he plunged his thumbnail into the pithy skin and squeezed its entire contents down his throat. It was then that he heard footsteps. He slipped the mashed-up orange into his jacket pocket and looked ahead. A small girl in bare feet came running up to him. She was wearing a torn, grey pinafore dress and a dirty white blouse. She couldn't have been more than eight or nine, and was clearly distressed. 'Sir, have you seen an orange heading this way?' 'No,' lied Ricky, licking the tangy residue from his lips. Her shoulders dropped. She said, 'They say my father is an illegal immigrant and tomorrow they will deport him to Albania. I went to Armley Prison tonight for one last hug but they turned me away. I stood outside the prison walls and shouted his name. Through the bars of his cell he blew me a final kiss and threw me an orange. But I stumbled on the sloping streets of this steep city and my orange has disappeared in the night.' Obviously she had a heavy

Albanian accent, almost unintelligible in fact, and for the sake of comprehension her remarks are paraphrased here. She fell to her knees and sobbed. 'What colour was it?' Ricky asked. At school, humour would often mitigate his wrongdoings. 'I wanted to eat every morsel of that orange, even the skin. Its juice was my father's blood and the flesh was his spirit,' said the girl. 'Why don't I help you search for it?' Ricky offered. The girl looked up at Ricky with a face like a silver coin at the bottom of a deep well caught by the momentary glimmer of a footman's lantern. 'No one can replace my father,' she said, 'but maybe one day someone will find it in their heart to care for me. A kind and honourable man. Someone like yourself.' A perfectly spherical tear trembled on her eyelash, and there was nothing Ricky could do to stop his hand from wiping that tear away, as if all humanity were pulling on a puppet string connected to his wrist. As his sticky hand neared her face, her nostrils flared at the scent of the orange. Then her eyes widened as she saw the fleshy strands of fruit clinging to his fingers and thumb. She said, 'Sir, was that my orange?' Ricky knew there was a great deal riding on his answer. It was like chaos theory: the wrong word here and the tremor would be felt all across Europe. Quick as a flash he produced the mangled fruit from his pocket. 'This?' he said. 'Do you mean this? Oh, no, no, no. In England we call these apples. This is an apple. Try saying it after me. Apple. Apple.'

The Knack

Boris was sitting in a field of bullocks above the house where he'd lived as a boy, trying to be a writer. There were many wild flowers waiting patiently to be described. But every time his pen made contact with the paper his hand skidded and jumped. Boris had to wonder about the spasms; were they the onset of epilepsy or some terrible motor-function illness? Or variant CJD perhaps – he'd certainly eaten a lot of dubious meat dishes in his younger years, including a cow's brain and also a cow's heart, though not at the same meal. However, this sudden loss of muscle control wasn't in any way unpleasant, in fact it felt a bit trippy, and after a time he gave up fighting it and let the pen wander at will. And although arbitrary, the peaks and troughs it produced had a confidence about them, something you couldn't argue with, like a cross-section of the Alps or a graph of Romany populations over the centuries. Eventually Boris found himself quite detached from his notepad, gazing down at the small end-terrace, at the frosted window of the bathroom where his handsome father had handed him his first disposable razor. 'The knack,' said his father, 'is to . . .' But his advice on shaving was drowned out by the siren which blared from the roof of the village fire station, and the old man bolted from the house, racing along the road on his bicycle, jumping from bike to fire engine like a bareback rider switching horses at the circus, heading for the mushroom of black smoke mushrooming over a distant town. And there he entered the Inferno. Boris put his hand to his throat. The flowers were still waiting. Then James Tate, a poet much admired in America, went by in an autogyro, flicking Boris the V-sign. *North* America, I should say, though for all I know he might be the toast of Tierra del Fuego, and a household name in Bogotá.

The Practical Way to Heaven

The opening of the new exhibition space at the Sculpture Farm had been a wonderful success. 'Would all those visitors returning to London on the 3:18 from Wakefield Westgate please make their way to the main entrance from where the shuttle bus is about to depart,' announced a nasaly Maggie over the PA system. She'd been having trouble with her adenoids. The London people put down their wine glasses and plates and began to move through the concourse. 'Great show, Jack,' said Preminger, helping himself to a final goat's cheese tartlet and a skewered Thai prawn. 'And not a pie in sight!' 'Thanks for coming,' said Jack. 'Put that somewhere for me, will you?' said Preminger, passing Jack his redundant cocktail stick before shaking hands and marching off towards the coach. A proud and happy man, Jack asked his staff, all eight of them, to assemble in the cafeteria, and he thanked them for their effort. 'Have all the Londoners gone?' he asked Maggie. 'Yes,' she said through her nose, peering out of the window as the back wheels of the bus rattled over the cattle grid. 'Very good. So here's your reward,' said Jack. He clapped his hands, and in through the double doors of the kitchen came Bernard driving a forklift truck, and on it, the most enormous pie. A wild, ecstatic cheer reverberated among the tables and chairs. 'Fill your wellies!' cried Jack. Tina from the gift shop could not restrain herself; she ripped off a section of the crust, dunked her arm in as far as her elbow, and smeared her face with rich brown gravy. Seth the gardener wasn't far behind, gnashing frenziedly at the crimped edging, followed by Millicent from publicity who hooked out a juicy piece of steak, went down on all fours and gorged on it like a starving dingo. Soon everyone was devouring the pie. And like all the great pies of history, the more they ate, the bigger it became. Jack threw his jacket into the corner of the room and whipped off his shirt and trousers. He was wearing blue swimming trunks. Standing on the rim of the metal dish he lowered himself through the light pastry topping. Maggie followed suit in her bra and pants, until all the staff of the Sculpture Farm were rolling or wading or lolling or lazing or helping themselves in the great slow pool of the pie. Now the forklift doubled as a diving board as Bernard bellyflopped from one of its prongs into the warm mush. It was only after retrieving a baby carrot from between his toes that Jack looked up and saw Preminger, who'd forgotten his wallet. 'You people,' he seethed. His face looked like the smell of a broken sewer in high summer. Jack stood up. 'I can explain everything,' he said. A chunk of braised celery slithered over his sternum. Preminger spluttered, 'You told me the pie thing was over. Finished. You said it was safe in the north, Jack Singleton. But look at you. Call yourself a Sculpture Farmer? You couldn't clean out a hamster cage.' 'Forgive us,' said Jack. 'We're pie people. Our mothers and fathers were pie people, and their mothers and fathers before them. Pies are in our blood.' 'Don't tell it to me. Tell it to them,' said Preminger, pointing to the window. On the other side of the glass stood the idling coach. Like a row of gargoyles, the faces of critics, sponsors, trustees, rich benefactors and famous names from the world of animal art looked out disgusted and appalled. Preminger swivelled on his heel and exited. The bus revved and departed.

Leaving gravy footprints behind him, Jack wandered out of the building and into the landscape beyond. And the crocodile of staff followed him, past the iron pigs, up to the granite bull on the hill, then along by the pit pony carved in coal and the shimmering flock of stainless-steel geese in the far meadow. Finally they found themselves in a small temple in the woods, with tea lights on the stone steps, the flames of which looked like the sails from a flotilla of tiny yachts in a distant bay. Torches to each corner of the building burned with an imperial pride. In front of Jack, soaked in pie juice, stood his loyal staff: Jethro with his three fingers; Maggie with her shopping problem; Tina who'd fallen in a quarry; Conrad who'd done time. Jack said, 'In the horse I see the plough, in the bull I see the wheel, in the goat I see the scythe, in the pig I see the stove. Bernard,' he shouted into the shadowy woods behind them, 'bring out the custard.'

To the Bridge

The same bridge, in fact, where it had occurred to
him that the so-called Manic Street Preachers, for all
their hyperventilation and sulphuric aftershave,
were neither frenzied, credible or remotely
evangelical, just as the so-called Red Hot Chili
Peppers, for all their encouraging ingredients, were
actually no warmer than a baby's bathwater and not
in the least bit *diablo*, whereas the Teardrop
Explodes, either by blind accident or through
careful purpose had kept every promise ever made.
Below him, the soupy canal acknowledged that final
thought with an anointing ripple then slouched
unknowingly yet profusely onwards.

Beyond Huddersfield

We drove a couple of hundred miles north. To sip beer in a log cabin. To taste the air from the mountains and feel the DNA of our ancestors tingle in our marrow. We hooked compliant fish from the lake, grilled them over a log fire and ate with our hands as the sun melted into the west. And on leaving, we left the place just as we'd found it: cleaned out the stove, swept the veranda, made a fingertip search of the meadow for the tiniest slivers of silver foil and suchlike, and folded the cold ashes into the earth. On the way south we pulled in at a roadside recycling site to offload the rubbish. The woman on the gate with the gun and the clipboard waved us over and said, 'Plastics in one, cans in two, cardboard and paper in three, and there's a bear in four, so mind how you go.' True enough, in the last skip, a black bear was squatting in a pile of junk. He was a sizeable creature and no mistake, could have creamed my head clean off with one swipe of those claws had the notion occurred. But he just sat there, on his throne of trash, doing nothing, staring his five mile stare.

In the days that followed I thought a lot about that bear. With every recollection he became more wretched and undignified in my mind, and I couldn't suppress the escalation of inglorious imagery. First he was begging with a paper cup. The next time I thought about him he was wearing a nylon housecoat. Then a pair of Ugg boots, and the tortilla wrap between his paws was a soiled nappy. Then he was flipping burgers with a floral lampshade on his head and a whitewall tyre around his neck, and the next weekend, either for his sake or mine, nothing could stop me jumping in the car after work and racing north to the tip. It

was two in the morning when I drew up. The gate was
locked but I hopped over, walked onto the gantry above the
dumping bays and shone a torch into the void. There he
was, asleep in the skip, snoring like a sawmill. But
swinging the car around to drive home the headlights made
one final sweep of the scene, and I saw him again, on his
hind legs now, the grapefruit in his mouth like a luminous
gumshield, pizza toppings and chicken bones hanging from
his matted coat, a red bandana knotted tightly around his
skinny thigh, leaning to his work, busy at his groin, the
gleaming needle digging for the sunken vein.

Cheeses of Nazareth

I fear for the long-term commercial viability of the new
Christian cheese shop in our neighbourhood. Poor old
Nathan, he's sunk every penny of his payout from the
Criminal Injuries Compensation Board into that place,
but to me the enterprise seems doomed. Last Friday he
had to make a trip across town to the opticians. 'Will you
mind the shop for me – I'll pay you, of course?' he said
'Nathan, it will be an honour to wear the smart blue
smock of the cheesemonger and to spend time amongst
such noble foodstuffs,' I replied. But in eight hours only
three people crossed the threshold of his emporium: some
knackered old dosser asking for a glass of water, a young
villain in bare feet looking for the needle exchange, and a
pregnant woman suddenly overwhelmed by a craving for
Kraft Cheese Slices, a product Nathan refuses to stock.
'Nathan, Nathan, Nathan, wouldn't this business have
been better suited to one of the more fashionable
districts? Is it too late to relocate?' He blinked at me
through his new specs. 'No, my work is here,' he said.
'Hope must put down its anchor even in troubled waters.
Today a cheese shop, tomorrow a wine bar or
delicatessen, next week a community centre or a
playground for the little ones, until ye church be builded.'
Then he went outside with a bucket of soapy water to
attack the graffiti scrawled across his front door.

I almost love Nathan for his dedication to the cause, but
the hour of my betrayal draws ever nearer. How did it
come to this, unemployed and lactose intolerant,
surrounded by expensive and rude-smelling dairy
products in a fleapit of a council flat during the hottest

summer on record? Pretty soon I'll have to turn my back
on Nathan, slip away like the last visitor in the lamplit
oncology ward withdrawing his hand from the weightless
grip of his mumbling mother-in-law. From up here on the
third floor I can see Nathan right now in his ironed apron
and starched hat. Nathan, oh Nathan, silent and alone,
presiding over the faceless faces of Camembert and Brie,
the millstones of Buterkäse and Zanetti Grana Padano,
the dried teardrop of San Simon, the uninhabited planets
of Gouda and Chaumes, and the cowpat of Cornish Yarg,
mummified in its drab nettle-leaf skin.

Show and Tell

Marlon said, 'That was the school on the phone. They
want me to go in and talk to Jennifer's class.' 'You?
Why you? You don't know shit about shit,' said his
significant other. 'All the other dads have done it. They
say it's my turn.' 'Well, you'd better not make a pig's
arse of it, for your precious little Jenny's sake. But don't
ask me, I'm only the wicked stepmother,' she said. Then
she went back to her online taxidermy lesson.

For the next week or so Marlon was in a muck sweat,
fretting about the talk he'd agreed to give. Finally he
decided a quick show-and-tell session should do the trick.
Something to focus their attention – concentrate their
minds. The morning duly arrived, and although Marlon
had visited the school on several occasions, today the
route seemed unfamiliar and through a part of town far
rougher than he remembered. After bottoming the car
on a truly formidable sleeping policeman he pulled up
at a barrier. A man in a serge blue uniform spoke to him
from behind the metal grille of a fortified kiosk. 'ID,'
he said. Marlon scrambled for his driving licence in the
glove compartment. 'I've come to talk to Class 9.' 'Sign
this disclaimer,' said the guard, then pointed the way
without removing his gauntlet. As instructed, Marlon
parked up, passed through a metal detector then followed
a line of dried blood splashes to a room at the end of a
basement corridor. Halfway along he spotted his daughter,
who took one look at him – especially at his shoes – and
bolted. Inside the classroom about twenty young teenagers
were sprawled across tables and chairs, scratching and
yawning. Thinking that surprise was his best tactic,

Marlon gulped down a big breath of air, fetched a small rust-coloured stone out of his pocket and said, 'Has anyone here ever seen a shooting star? Has anyone ever held a piece of outer space in their hand? Does anyone know what this is?' A boy at the back in a stabproof body warmer put his hand up. 'What's your ride, man?' 'Excuse me?' said Marlon. 'What kind of car do you drive, granddad?' said the boy. 'A Clio,' Marlon told him. 'That's a pussy's car,' said the boy, and the whole class sniggered. Marlon was still holding the stone between his thumb and index finger, but awkwardly, like a robot picking up an egg. Another boy with a swastika tattoo on his earlobe strolled right up to Marlon and said, 'Have you got any money, or no?' 'Not on me,' lied Marlon. 'Come on, we're wasting our time with this muppet,' said the young Nazi. With their hands rammed in their pockets the rest of the class followed him out of the room. Only a petite, bespectacled girl remained in her seat. She was very tiny indeed – just a dot of a thing. In a voice like the squeaking wheel of a pram she said, 'That's no meteorite. It's just a pebble you picked up on the road. Isn't it, mister? Isn't it?' Marlon said, 'Do you know my daughter, Jennifer?' 'You're not Jenny's dad. Jenny's dad's got no legs,' she piped. Marlon wasn't crying exactly, but behind his eyes tears were streaming like rain down the windows of an all-night café. 'Look, I'll show you the way to the caretaker's office then you'll have to make a run for it,' said the girl. 'But it'll have to look like there's been a struggle. A black eye at least, and maybe a broken nose, just to be safe.' Marlon thought about the brittle, porcelain cheekbones beneath the pale skin of her face. 'I could never hit a child,' he said. 'Stupid – it's me whacking you,' she said, pulling a telescopic truncheon out of her book bag. Marlon turned away from the blow. Just then Jennifer's face appeared in the panel of safety glass in the classroom door. Suddenly the meteorite started to glow.

Upon Unloading the Dishwasher

Even though Katy was desperate to end her affair with
Raymond she agreed to a rendezvous at a local gallery.
Standing in front of a canvas onto which the blood of a
dead rabbit had dripped and congealed, Raymond said,
'It's kind of rabbit-shaped – do you think that's the point?'
When she didn't answer, Raymond raised his voice. 'I
SAID IT'S KIND OF RABBIT-SHAPED – DO YOU
THINK THAT'S THE POINT?' When Katy finally replied,
here's what she said:

'Raymond, imagine my surprise when, upon unloading
the dishwasher, I discovered the image of The World's
Most Wanted Man imprinted on one of my best dinner
plates. I phoned the Customer Service Hotline. This bored-
sounding operative somewhere in the subcontinent said to
me, "So let me get this straight, madam, you've found The
World's Most Wanted Man taking refuge in your
dishwasher?" "No," I said, and explained again in plain
English. He said, "Are you sure it isn't a gravy stain or the
residue from a pork chop? Meat products can be very
stubborn, and for heavy soiling we recommend a pre-soak.
Also, you might want to try a longer cycle at a higher
temperature, and can I ask which type of detergent you're
using? Is it tablet or sachet?" Then maybe he heard my
sobbing because he said, "OK, we'll send somebody
round." Five minutes later there was a knock at the door
and in came a policeman and a priest. "That's him all right,"
said the officer, holding the dinner plate up to the light and
confirming the identity of The World's Most Wanted Man.
"Is it a miracle?" I asked. The priest had closed his eyes
and was sitting on the pedal bin with his arms folded

across his chest. The policeman laughed. "Are you kidding – this is the ninth this week. And it isn't just plates. It's cups, dishes, ice cubes, toast, pizzas. A woman in Hull found him in a wholemeal loaf, all the way through." Then he said, "We'll have to take this appliance away, get the lab boys to give it the once-over." Now I was crying again. I said, "But it's Christmas Eve. I've got a party of twelve to cater for tomorrow, including Dr Roscoe and that poor boy who stands in the park all day flipping a coin. What shall I do?" He said, "At times like this some people find that praying helps." With his extendable baton he pointed at a place on the lino where I might kneel. I asked him if he'd join me, but he replied, "I won't, if you don't mind. Like my old man told me, there are only two reasons for putting your hands together: one's for ironic applause, the other's to scrub up before dinner, and even then the palms don't actually touch because they're separated by an invisible and infinitely thin film of detergent. What you call soap.'"

Every word that Katy had uttered was complete poppycock. She knew it and Raymond knew it too. But the security guard had gone outside for a cigarette, and they were the only living souls left in the great, echoing hangar of the gallery. And Katy knew with an absolute clarity of perception that the moment she stopped talking the fresh and bloody wound of Raymond's mouth would move quickly and incisively against her own.

Poodles

They all looked daft but the horse-dog looked
daftest of all. The cute red bridle and swishing
tail, the saddle and stirrups, the groomed mane.
The hair round its feet had been shaved and
fluffed into hooves. Close up, on its hind, there
were vampire bites where the clippers had steered
too close to the skin. Skin that was blotchy and
rude. I leaned over the rail and whispered,
'You're not a horse, you're a dog.' It bared its
canines and growled: 'Shut the fuck up, son. Forty-
five minutes and down come the dirty bombs – is
that what you want? Now offer me one of those
mints and hold it out in the flat of your hand.
Then hop on.' I was six, with a kitten's face and
the heart of a lamb.

The Personal Touch

My cohabitee can be pretty demanding. Asked what she
wanted for our first anniversary she replied, 'I want some
space, Paul, and plenty of it.' I said, 'Are you absolutely
sure? You wouldn't rather have a macramé seat cover
for the Mercedes Roadster I bought you for Christmas?
Or one of those metallic-coloured MP3 players I saw you
admiring over at Brett's house the other day?' She put
aside her nail file and said, 'Paul, space is what I want
and space is what I need. Do I have to SPELL IT OUT?'

I went down to the hardware shop in the high street. It
was very manly in there, lots of stern objects made from
uncompromising metals. Lots of 'big ticket' items with
throttles and interchangeable blades. 'Got any space?'
I asked the man in the brown overalls. 'Sure,' he said.
'What kind of thing were you looking for? Doesn't come
cheap, mind.' He showed me some second-hand space
they were letting go for half price, but one lot appeared
somewhat dog-eared around the edges, and another batch
had been wallpapered with woodchip during the '70s, and
yet another carried a vague whiff of embalming fluid. He
pulled down a huge pattern book and showed me the
entire range: hexagonal space, deep ocean space, space
that glowed in the dark, vacuum-packed space, space that
had been brought back from outer space, space that
giggled when you poked it, space made out of air bubbles
extracted from core samples of Antarctic ice dating back
billions of years. I just couldn't decide. The shopkeeper
said, 'It's for a lady friend, right?' I couldn't even bring
myself to nod – my head felt like a famous but forgotten
church bell sitting in a scrap yard on the wrong side of

the river. He said, 'In which case, let me recommend this. It's pretty neutral, standard spec., no trimmings to speak of, but in a situation like your own I always think it's better to play safe.' I went for a haircut while he gift-wrapped the space, then in the newsagents I bought a gift tag in the shape of a serenading starfish, and wrote on it, 'Here's what you asked for, my sweetheart. I only hope it's enough.' I dropped the package on the doorstep and pressed the buzzer. Then I zoomed off in the Roadster, faster than I'd ever travelled in my whole existence, straight along Quarry Road.

The Last Panda

Unprecedented economic growth in my native country
has brought mochaccino and broadband to where there
was nothing but misery and disease, yet with loss of
habitat the inevitable consequence; even the glade I was
born in is now a thirty-storey apartment block with valet
parking and a nail salon. They scrape DNA from the
inside of my cheek and freeze it, 'just in case'. To the
world I'm known by my stage name and am Richard to
family and friends, but never Dick. Well-meaning
tourists visiting the Cavern throw pastries and pieces of
fruit despite notices regarding my sensitive nature and
strict diet. I cried all night when John was shot, rubbed
the tired circles of my eyes till they turned black. Please
do not tap on the glass. The sixties did it for everyone, I
mean EVERYONE, and what people failed to grasp
about Chairman Mao was that despite the drab-looking
suits and systematic violations of basic human rights
he liked a good tune as much as the next man.
Liverpool's a great shag but you wouldn't want to marry
it. They named a potato snack in my honour and also a
small family car, how many people can say that? Fans
write to me from as far away as Papua New Guinea and I
insist on responding personally. In fact my 'sixth digit' –
an enlarged wrist bone which functions as a thumb –
means that handwriting comes easier to me than it does to
many other creatures, for example the Rolling Stones. If
I didn't believe there was one more hit record in me I
swear I'd end it now. In the dream, there's still a Paul
and a George somewhere in the high valleys of Ganzu
Province, classic period white shirts and black ties, mop
tops down to their shoulders, strumming away. These

sunglasses have prescription lenses and are not just for
effect. Reviewing my Wikipedia entry I note that
'Yellow Submarine' and 'Octopus's Garden' anticipated
the absurdist trend in rock 'n' roll by at least a decade.
Every first Tuesday in the month the lady vet gives me a
hand job but due to the strength of the tranquilliser the
pleasure is all hers. Years ago they brought Yoko to the
doors of my cage but it wouldn't have worked; I let the
slow snowball of my head roll sadly eastwards and
stared towards the Himalayas. In the whole cosmos
there's only me. What hurts most isn't the loneliness
but the withering disrespect: as if they'd dropped a couple
of bamboo sticks into my paws and I'd just played along.

Sold to the Lady in the Sunglasses and Green Shoes

My girlfriend won me in a sealed auction but wouldn't
tell me how much she bid. 'Leave it, Frank. It's not
important. Now go to sleep,' she said. But I was restless.
An hour later I woke her and said, 'Give me a ballpark
figure.' 'I'm tired,' she replied. I put the light on. 'But
are we talking like thousands here?' She rolled away,
pulled the cotton sheet over her head, mumbling, 'You're
being silly, Frank.' I said, 'Oh, being silly am I? So not
thousands. Just a couple of hundred, was it?' 'I'm not
telling you, so drop it,' she snarled. By now I was wide
awake. 'Fifty, maybe? A tenner?' She didn't say anything,
and when Elaine doesn't say anything I know I'm getting
close to the truth. Like the other day with the weed killer.
I said, 'Maybe you weren't bidding for me at all. Maybe
you were after a flat-screen telly or a home sun-tanning
unit, and you got me instead. Tell me, Elaine. Tell me
what I'm worth, because right now I don't know if I'm
an original Fabergé? egg or just something the cat dragged
in.' Elaine surfaced from under the covers and took a sip
of water from the glass on the bedside table. 'Frank, listen.
What does it matter if it was a million pounds or a second-
class stamp? You're priceless, OK? You're everything to
me. Don't spoil it by talking about money.' Then she took
my hand and held it against her breast and said, 'Do you
want to make love?' I answered with my body, tipping
every last quicksilver coin into her purse.

But that night I dreamed of the boy-slave winning his
freedom by plucking a leaf from Diana's golden bough,
and long before dawn, with bread in my knapsack and
the wind at my back, I strode forth.

The War of the Roses

Mancunian Norman had just turned on to the M621 when he saw a pewter-haired old man in a brown suit sitting on a signpost, with his hands covering his face. He appeared to be sobbing. Being a thoughtful sort with a church upbringing and a diploma in sociology, Norman eased up then reversed slowly along the hard shoulder. He stepped out of the car and said, 'Couldn't help noticing how sad you looked. Can I give you a lift into the city?' The old man's face was soggy with tears, some of which had dripped onto his lapels, leaving black spots like air-pellet holes on the chocolate-coloured jacket. 'I'm sad all right,' he said. 'Did you read about the boy in the sewers?' Norman shook his head. 'Five days he was down there, his screams coming up through every drain and sink. I heard him myself one night when I was cleaning my teeth, and a more sorrowful noise I never knew. They sent in potholers. They sent in the Moorland Rescue. They even sent in Rentokil.' 'Did they find him?' asked Norman. 'Dragged him out through a manhole cover in Clay Pit Lane last night. The rats had got him. I don't think this city will ever be the same again.' Another tear dithered on the point of his chin then dripped onto his shoe. 'You seem to have taken it very hard,' observed Norman. 'Hit by a train,' said the man, 'and I'll show you why.' He stood up and pointed at the sign he'd been perching on. It read, *Welcome to Leeds. Population 715,403.* 'It's my job to keep this sign up to date. As soon as I heard about sewer boy's sorry demise I walked here over the meadows, swishing through the morning dew, with my pocket screwdriver and my bag of numbers.' He produced a scrunched-up Tesco's carrier from his jacket pocket. 'But when I looked there was no number two. I've got a five, I've got three sixes and an eight, but no two. And what am I if I can't dignify that boy's agonising demise with the right number? I'm a useless old gimmer and I'm going to hear his inconsolable wailing for ever.' 'Let me see,' said Norman, peering into the plastic bag. The old man was right. There was no number two. There was a half-eaten carrot and a wooden fish, but no number two. 'A couple of years ago a woman in Beeston had triplets. I walked here over the meadows, swishing through the morning dew with my pocket screwdriver and my bag of numbers, and the population that day stood at 715, 406. I had no number nine. And, well . . . I've never told anyone this before, I just swivelled that number six upside down. I'm not proud of what I did that day, but this is worse. This is shameful. It's going to haunt me to my grave.' 'Can't you buy new numbers?' said Norman, ever the pragmatist, always looking for a positive outcome. 'Not like these. These were made by the founding fathers, cast from the anchor of the first boat to pull up on the banks of our plentiful river. I should have guarded them with my life. But people borrow them and don't bring them back. The number one is on loan to a folk museum in Ottawa, and my grandson . . . he stole a few numbers and sold them to buy ketamine. Listen, do you hear crying? Do you hear that pitiful wail?' 'It's just the breeze in the overhead cables,' said Norman, and he helped the broken old man into the passenger seat of his car. They sat there not speaking for a few minutes, and the vehicle shook as articulated lorries rumbled past in the inside lane. The clouds started to clear and the streetlights went out. Then Norman said, 'I've got it. What if I come and live in Leeds, then the sign can stay as it is?' 'Would you do that for me? Really and truly?' asked the old man. 'Of course, no question,' said Norman.

Things started to move very rapidly. The old man directed him through the rush-hour traffic to an office at the back of the Calls Hotel. 'Sign here,' said the Registration Officer. Norman took a fountain pen from his briefcase and signed the form. It was official – he was now a citizen of 'The Knightsbridge of the North', as some commentators have called it. But when he turned around to shake hands, the pewter-haired man in the brown suit was high-fiving with councillor Bill Hyde, The Right Worshipful Lord Mayor of the City of Leeds. Then the doors flew open, and three policemen wearing canvas hoods dropped Norman to the ground, ripped open his shirt, and plunged a white-hot branding iron into his chest, just above his heart.

Norman lives in Roundhay now, not far from the park. I doubted him once, and asked him to show me the proof. He parted his dressing gown and I read the words *Leeds, Like It Or Lump It* seared into his ageing flesh. Then he hobbled to the window and looked at the hills to the west. To the Pennines, if my geography is correct, or, as they're sometimes known, 'The Great Divide'.

A Nativity

We're heading up to bed, Mary and I, drawing the
curtains against the cold, inquisitive night, turning
down the wick, setting up the fireguard to cage the
sleeping tiger in the grate. Mary is just about to sweep
the line of toy animals into the shoe box, where they
live, when I say, 'Just for once, shall we leave them
where they lie?' Mary hesitates and says, 'You mean
right here? On the floor? Underfoot?' I kneel down on
the rug. On closer inspection they're all dogs – moulded
plastic, mainly, but a few made from china or pot, and
a couple of border collies cast in iron or lead. Mary
kneels also, and we notice in detail the many breeds, the
great variety of shape and form. The Pekinese lifting its
wounded paw; the shiny-nosed spaniel; the Scottie dog
with the scarlet collar and erect tail; the yappy terrier
baiting the foursquare St Bernard; the sleek red setter
with a juicy bone in its mouth; the line of Dalmatian
pups, six, no seven in total, all nose to tail.

And crouching low behind them we see their purpose,
their procession, how they journey as one towards the
towering green mountain of the Christmas spruce,
where baubles are small villages among the wooded
slopes, and fairy lights are streetlamps on the narrow
path zigzagging its way to the starry summit. Mary
says, 'You're so right. We should leave them as they
are, tonight and every night. Think of his thrilled face
in dawn's tender glow.' Then we climb the ladder to
the loft and bed down together in the loose feathers
and straw, exultant with our choice, creators of a new
tomorrow, peacemakers in the holy war.

The Delegates

At the annual Conference of Advanced Criminal Psychology,
Dr Amsterdam and myself skipped the afternoon seminar on
Offending Behaviours Within Gated Communities and went
into town to go nicking stuff. In Halfords he pilfered a shiny
aluminium gizmo for measuring the tread depth on a car tyre
and I nabbed a four-digit combination lock. In the gardening
section of John Lewis's he filched a Butterflies of the British
Countryside Wallchart while I pocketed a squirrel-proof bird
feeder. In Poundstretcher he whipped a small tin of Magic
Stain Remover and I helped myself to a signed 2005 official
McFly calendar. In Specsavers he purloined a pair of silver-
rimmed varifocals and I lifted an origami snowflake from the
window display. In Waterstone's he slipped an unauthorised
biography of disgraced South African cricket captain Hansie
Cronje inside his raincoat and I sneaked out with an Original
Magnetic Poetry Kit. In Oxfam he appropriated a five-
hundred-piece Serengeti at Dusk jigsaw and I swiped a set of
six coasters designed by authenticated aborigines. Then with
our laminated delegate passes streaming over our shoulders
on lanyards of pink and purple ribbon we legged it out of the
precinct and across the park. And from the high iron bridge
we slung the lot over the ornate railings into the filthy river
below until every last item of merchandise had either sunk
without trace or was drifting away downstream. 'Remind
me, Stephen, why we do this,' said Dr Amsterdam. I said,
'I really don't recall.' Peeling a brown calfskin glove from
the cold, moulded fingers of his prosthetic hand he said,
'Let's make this our last, shall we?' We shook on the deal,
and even managed a partial embrace. A mute swan pecked
idly at a Paisley-patterned chiffon scarf before it picked up
speed and slithered over the weir.

The Overtones

When you ask me what time it is, it's purple. And when
the alarm goes off in a morning it's a sort of metallic, minty
green, like the noisette triangle in a packet of Quality Street
– a particular favourite of mine but hard on the teeth. And
when you love me, and whisper your love for me,
personally, into my inner ear, it's custard-yellow embossed
with a bold red heart, like a door I once saw in an otherwise
dried-up town on the side of a hill near Salamanca.
Salamanca, which is beige but burnt at the edges. Most
days I'm here on the other side of the glass, under the high
ceilings. It's like a job, but without the bit you call work.
In prison, I'd be the one pushing the trolley of books along
the corridors, recommending cowboy adventure stories to
big-time embezzlers, making the Arc de Triomphe out of
toothpicks, cave-painting the walls of his cell. If you're
passing, ring the bell of the studio and come up. This
morning I'm tackling some major piece, but where to start?
There's no instruction book for an activity of this nature, no
downloadable manual. With a domestic knife I pop open a
tin of True Confessions and tip it out on the canvas, thick
treacly jollops, but another tone is needed in this top corner
so I go for a touch of Wednesday Week, which you might
be surprised to learn was the colour of Caesar's pillow and
whose essence is obtained from the pituitary gland of the
ocelot. What next? How about a little Male Model, to
echo that thin trace of Mars Bars bottom left. The
telephone wants feeding in the back office but it will have
to wait. Now for some softer hues: a daub of Julie Ocean
should do the trick when combined with this swatch of
onion sack. Did I shave this morning or was that the day
before? See, sometimes I'm Don Quixote tilting at

imaginary foes. Sometimes I'm Casanova planting a final kiss on the peach-like breast of the Contessa before leaping from the balcony into a waiting gondola, her volcano-faced husband flailing at my shadow with his leather fist. And sometimes I'm more like myself, black coffee hardening in a cup, seagulls caterwauling in the bay, my hands too big for their cuffs. That pretty trawler in the lee of St Michael's Mount is a Radio 4 afternoon play about a working-class boy who raised a lion cub under his bed: note how easy it is for the mind to nod off at the tiller, but frankly that's the idea. So before I know it I've piped a delicate line of My Perfect Cousin around a triangle of ripstop with all the precision of the master cake decorator applying a blushing smile to his icing-sugar bride. My darling, if I embedded a long, moon-coloured sliver of your priceless hair beneath this thick blob of Jimmy Jimmy, could it be our secret till our dying breath? Runaround, Here Comes the Summer, It's Going to Happen – properly blended they form the most eye-catching shade but one yet to be named. Acrylics summon me to the dancefloor! Sure, these paintings are loud, but do I look like a mouse? It's chaos in here but a kind which I understand and call home. There must always be a small corner of rapture, otherwise what's the point? And all the while I'm tapping my feet to the colours, going at it with brushes or blades until the world looks for all the world like it sounds.

The Sighting of the Century

During the summer of 1996 I was working as a Tattooist-in-Residence on a reclaimed slagheap in the South Pennines. On July 28th at three minutes past midday I was approached by Mary-Anne Nogan (M-AN) and her then husband Mark Dawson (MD), who reported an unusual sighting near the disused pithead. Locking up the kiosk, we travelled in their Citroën Saxo to within a hundred yards or so of the site, then cut the engine and freewheeled down the slope in relative silence. No sooner had we engaged the handbrake than I knew with almost one hundred per cent certainty that we were looking at a juvenile female Celebrity (*Movie Star*). As misfortune would have it, local landslip and subsidence have caused something of a dead-spot for mobile phone coverage in a region otherwise lush with signal, and I dispatched MD on foot to 'get on the jungle drums' from the nearest public phone in a local hamlet. The celebrity had taken up position on a cantilevered metal girder about twenty yards or so in front of us, and despite being a good three thousand miles off the beaten track seemed relatively unperturbed. The defining features I would summarise as follows: a slim-bodied celebrity with enhanced features, conspicuously plumper than a stonechat. Its song I would describe as a repetitive me me *me*, me me *me*, and in behaviour it displayed the frequent 'coquettish' flicking of the rump and strutting walk so closely associated with the species. Being entirely unprepared for such a wholly unexpected sighting, we possessed no photographic equipment, not even a notepad and pencil to make a rough field sketch. However, I remembered that in my knapsack I always carried a reserve tattoo kit along with a basic selection of coloured inks. I hooked the electric needle up to the car battery, and M-AN made the ultimate sacrifice when, without being asked, she lifted her blouse over her head, uncoupled the clasp of her bra strap and offered the unblemished surface of her bare back as a canvas. MD returned, scarlet-faced and out of breath, and after a few words of explanation on my part he agreed I should carry on with the sketch, and even contributed himself to the outlining of the secondary feathers with a blue biro from his pocket. It wasn't long before several members of the local Celebrity Spotters Club were on the scene, and only hours before other twitchers had joined us from as far away as Manchester and Fridaythorpe. The celebrity continued to show well for four more days, even drawing observers from abroad, all keen to be present at what the *Yorkshire Evening Post* subsequently described as 'the sighting of the century'. And at a low-key but very moving ceremony near the pithead this summer, M-AN and myself unveiled a plaque carved in anthracite, dedicated to the memory of her former husband. A devoted father and keen amateur dentist, MD was to meet his untimely death in a freak drystone walling accident just six months after the extraordinary happenings of that extraordinary day.

The Crunch

I put on weight at Christmas, then more during
Lent. I tried the Nine Plums a Day Diet, the
Pine Needle Diet, then the Eat Your Way to
Health and Happiness with Pencil Shavings
and Talc Plan, then ate nothing but road salt
and hen feathers for more than a month, but just
piled it on, pound after pound. Each morning,
as naked as a fish and fully shaved, I gawped at
the digital readout on the bathroom scales, much
as a bereaved dog-lover might stare at a
veterinary bill.

My girlfriend was tactfully mute until
Valentine's night. After crawling out from
under the ruins of sex she led me by the
manacles through the wardrobe door, and there,
amongst hangers and rails, guided my fingers
towards tailored waistbands and handcrafted
belts, towards beautifully finished collars and
cuffs, towards the pinpoint darning of zips and
buttons and studs. Tearful in the hard,
indigenous light of the moon she whispered, 'If
you can't do it for me, then at least for these
attractive trousers, mister, or this handsome
jacket, or this gorgeous shirt?'

Bringing It All Back Home

I was doing what we've all done at some point in our lives, let's face it, Googling my own name, when I dropped across a website promoting the Cuckoo Day Festival in the village where I was born and grew up. Attractions included the Crowning of the Turnip King, the Dead Fish Throwing Competition, Worm Charming on the bowling green, an Armed Manhunt across the moor in pursuit of a well-known car thief, the Wheelbarrow Parade, and the opportunity to pelt a Tory councillor with out-of-date meat products. But the event which really caught my eye was the Simon Armitage Trail, a guided tour which promised to take in 'every nook and cranny of the poet's youth'. I went straight down to the local joke shop and bought myself a false wig-and-beard combination, completed the disguise with a large overcoat, and on the day of the tour made my way to the old lych gate at the appointed hour.

The turnout was woundingly low: two elderly ladies, three day trippers who'd missed the coach to Malham Cove, and some goofy-looking student with a notepad and pen in his hand. Our guide for the day was wearing a safari outfit, including khaki shorts and a bullwhip tucked in his belt. 'My name's Bob and thank you for coming,' said Bob, reading from his notes. 'And it's not just for convenience that we rendezvous beneath the eaves of this churchyard building. For it was here, acting as a pallbearer at his great-grandfather's funeral, that Armitage felt the weight of the coffin biting into his shoulder, and whose pain and subsequent tears were mistaken for grief by other mourners, an experience recounted in his first ever published poem, "The Black Lie".' The goofy student said,

'That explains the uncertainty of tone in that poem, the sense of loss which is actually an expression of guilt.' 'Exactly,' said Bob. One of the day trippers raised his hand and said, 'Can you tell me how long this is going to take? We thought we might try to catch the ferret juggling at midday.' 'Not long,' said Bob, 'it's not like we're talking Samuel Laycock here, right?' Adopting what I hoped was a Russian accent I cleared my throat and said, 'Are you sure about the lych gate story? Armitage could only have been a toddler when that funeral took place.' Bob said, 'Look, pal, don't start splitting hairs today, all right? I'm only standing in for my wife. When it comes to Simon Armitage she really knows her onions, but her brother's gone down with the shingles – big scabs right around his middle like a boxer's belt – so she's playing Florence Nightingale in Market Harborough while muggins here is left holding the baby. So don't shoot the messenger. I was supposed to be supervising the Bouncy Castle. Anyway, where do you come from?' 'Moscow,' I said, then added, 'Actually a small town about twenty miles to the east,' intending to give the falsehood a kind of detailed veracity. Bob said, 'OK, folks, if Leonid Brezhnev here hasn't got any more questions, let's move on.'

We walked up to the stagnant canal, where, according to Bob, my pet Yorkshire terrier had drowned while retrieving a tennis ball. Bob said, 'Armitage never got over that dog, and the whole sorry incident is recorded in his sonnet "Man's Best Friend". Who knows, maybe he should have gone in himself instead of sending that poor mutt to its death.' 'Presumably that explains some of the emotional retardation in his later work,' said the goofy student, whose front teeth were getting longer by the minute. 'Exactly,' said Bob. We waited for one of the day trippers, who'd wandered off along the towpath to read a noticeboard about horse-drawn barges in the nineteenth century, then the tour continued. With Bob spouting his stuff at every lamppost, we walked to a dilapidated cowshed where I was gored by a bull when I was nine, supposedly, then to the escarpment where I'd seen my father bring down a fieldfare with a single stone. Then to Bunny Wood where I'd found Gossip John hanging by the neck, then to a meadow where I'd fallen asleep and woken up with a grass snake curled on my chest, then behind the undertaker's parlour, where, Bob confidently announced, I'd lost my virginity to a girl called Keith. The two ladies tittered behind their hands. We wandered in a big circle for a couple of hours before arriving in the park, and congregated around the bronze, life-size statue of Simon Armitage. 'Of course it caused a huge stink at the time,' said Bob, lighting a cigarette and tossing the spent match into the bandstand. 'It looks like something to be proud of,' I said, from behind my beard. Bob rounded on me: 'Oh really? Well maybe that's how it looks from the Kremlin, but as it happens a lot of people in this village said the money should have gone to the Children's Hospice instead. Those kids with their big eyes and shaved heads – breaks your heart. But don't ask me, I'm only a taxpayer.' Goofy said, 'And once Armitage had packed his bags for Los Angeles he never came back.' 'Exactly so, son, exactly so,' said Bob. Then with the tip of his cigarette he pointed towards the white splodge on Armitage's scalp and the white streaks on his metal face and said, 'But at least the seagulls like it.' And everyone laughed. Bob said, 'All right, people, that just about wraps it up.' 'But what about the house, the Simon Armitage Homestead Experience?' I wanted to know. Bob sighed, impatiently. 'OK, Boris, take the keys and post them back through the letterbox when you're done. It's the one at the top of the hill with the broken windows. There's a compulsory donation of five pounds and be sure to wear the plastic overshoes. And don't touch a thing – it's just as he left it.' I said, 'You mean with the tin of mustard powder on the kitchen table, and a line of his father's ironed shirts hanging from the picture rail, the fancy ones that he wore on stage. And a folded newspaper propped on the arm of the chair, the cryptic crossword laddered with blue ink. And his mother's reading glasses, one arm folded the other outstretched, next to the silver pen?' Bob said, 'You tell me, you're the expert, Mr First Monkey in Space. Now, if you don't mind, I want to see Martin Amis opening the Duck Race, and we're running late.'

Last Day on Planet Earth

Lippincott takes a photograph with his eye.
Wittmann paints in the crust of salt with a
finger of spit. Yoshioka wheels the last
piano onto the fire. Owens throws stones at
a rock. The afternoon turns over in its sleep,
then sleeps.

Kirszenstein trades her kingfisher skull for
a tinned peach. Jerome traps air in a screw-
top jar. Bambuck plants the last of his teeth.
Johnson dresses his gangrenous wound with
a carrier bag. Bolt pulls up the ladder,
secures the hatch.